in field latin

THE
SEAGULL
LIBRARY OF
GERMAN
LITERATURE

in field latin

lutz seiler

TRANSLATED BY ALEXANDER BOOTH

LONDON NEW YORK CALCUTTA

 **GOETHE INSTITUT**

This publication was supported by a grant
from the Goethe-Institut India

Seagull Books, 2021

Originally published as Lutz Seiler, *im felderlatein*

© Suhrkamp Verlag, Berlin, 2010

First published in English translation by Seagull Books, 2015

Translation © Alexander Booth, 2015

ISBN 978 0 8574 2 834 9

British Library Cataloguing-in-Publication Data
A catalogue record for this book is available from the British Library

Typeset by Seagull Books, Calcutta, India
Printed and bound by WordsWorth India, New Delhi, India

contents

departure

bed against window, the trip
into the wood, ever more softly
shifting gears & sleep: every

dream begins uphill, at the fence
        onto the street where
someone squats like you, where

the resinous poppy with its
capsules clings to your ears, where
above already blossom edges have

gone to grey . . . leaf
after leaf put into place
& uncompleted sent away.

without a sound, that's
how we sang. & in the darkness even
closed our eyes.

there were parts of places, places

I

the new empire

telephonerustle, birdcough: first you go
through everything again in your thoughts; the
blue waffle tiles were there before, chest-high

the brown pedestal, oil &
shrubbery motif: shedding, almost
    music the
trickling forth of voices from
out of the ball lamps. no
labyrinth & no chandos-hysteria just

      the smell of words & fake carnations: in
the past this window wasn't barred, wasn't
marked with this script *come in*
to the research park they say is dead—herringbonetrim

II

there were parts of places, places

that i didn't know, never even
knew by name. there was
only one street &

a number for every house with
half a bow—
the lantern. within its beam

hung small, singable pieces *almost for free*
above the way & chalk
for one's voice. static, the patience

of resistance, the crackling into
life-threads. i
walked into its sound

& it silenced: animal-
like i held my skull up
to the moon, half-

open mouth & sightless—this
is how the province nourishes me. down
from its chutes cabled

names tumble, words still warm
on the tongue like *brizke*
dettloff kaatz . . . poetry

is only a blinking, spitting, moving on; storm-track
of lanternways

III

the rough tone

who thought *to the core*? i saw
    my footsteps
disappear, beaten, writing-hand pale

in the halls of bureaucracy: the inner core
is medium blue, a bird that
doesn't know how to go on turns soft, the

    rough tone, as if
a long breath slowly grinding
through your body; the moon

rising, fully aware of
its rarity, a milk tooth
lost before its time. behind it

a footprint, hooves
pull in the support-hills of the earth, the little tune
'the gravel rock' ticks above the stepping stones

right up to the house. it clicks nearby, scratches your heart
with rubber soles, sand now
underfoot . . . in imagined beatings i called out

    shake the light
from your caps maybe, but you
will not be greeted here

IV

when you have the benefit of hindsight

why all the same i like
to come here: it's the cold
on the eyes, impression-less places which

scatter one's glance: *houses*, *trees*, *cattle*—sunk
into the sound
of another plot. there

it's not really an i that speaks, it's
the small soft fingertips which
grow out alongside the doors, it's

the doves' scissor-like wings
which push their ribcages out & yet
still they climb, slowly,

with tucked feet; when
you have the benefit of hindsight
it could be the day's last light

upon the bird's chest. from
cornerstone to cornerstone the chaff
of its shadow springs, lines upon which

the dead's voices ring. when
you have the benefit of hindsight they breathe directly in-
to your face: lodger, house-book keeper, aranka, who

sang from out of the hollows of her knees . . . you
must meditate your own bones again, kommata
in the syntax of this region

V
sentry duty

i have said
something, sung without
my hands: i have

smoked up all the shadows.
lungward i took these shafts to where
the empty space begins the rustling
    out along the paling
towards the railway cars—seventeen years

before the text. in snowdust rolling over
bottles crap & the remains of masks where
the stillness stiffly marches
    past with
short swift shudders

into its own doing

VI

in the evening

animals trailed behind me floating
over the tracks. some
held their mouths ajar, just

over the earth & pitched
their breath into the oily grass—isolated
clumps stubborn like children's heads

growing up out of the rubble. i saw
how the turning-to-stone begins: for ever
about the ears. some solidified

with the rustling of the trees. some
suddenly snapped their skulls
into their necks & reared, a

black-hearted moon
between their hooves

VII

after the game

after the game maybe
it rained. the aluminium hooks glimmered, below
them lay the notches, legible

in the base, coated
with oil. up above
their sweaty half-moon shoulders

when a breath: some players
sat there quietly, with
crooked legs & gazed

out of the window. their hands got bigger
& grew heavy. i saw
the traces that slowly

shed from the soles of their shoes, a hundred
metres behind the site—the
billets broken open, the cabin doors

unclosed. there
wasn't a one who didn't
want to disappear, still

no one was absent without a reason
& everyone knew where he was

VIII
leftopenness

house-rows, half-floors—
at first you don't believe
how distant each movement is. the

longer they are out of time
places stand better still &
care: *come here*, *head*

high, you hear, the glass
crunches softly, pieces, shards, the birds'
short stuttering sobs

in the parquet which means: *chin*
up. that which
lasts you hear

through the stones. what
is to come, they say, as if
from out of nothing, that's how far

away it is

IX
before the demolition

before the demolition a
definitive pause, the clearing-away. the
spoken distances itself &

falls silent. a small
powdery human smell
springs up, set free from the house

he strikes his cane at the leaves.
his trough marked by
laughter, the eyes'

circumstances
highly flammable—the flick-
ering of hands

over the earth, their peal
through the air; a going going
into awkwardness

hand-wonder & diary

everything about me

there was a time when very slowly
with my ears from out
of the rain i came, saw rain
& could think of rain.

like oil gods
the old motors would crawl
out behind the hill &
the harvest began. i

would stick my arms deep
into the grain, would press
the seeds between my fingers &
had to close my eyes.

down from the beam hung a thin
skim of fat upon which the dead
flies slept &

in the hollow mould of the walls
hovered a child who
would call on me. he knew
everything about me

harvest fest

our luftwaffe! my grandfather would bellow
& therewith pull his scythe
across the sky. a pair
of these shimmering arcs was all it took & all

became connected: israel, the oak for peace, his
beloved horses (seized in sixty-one, for
valuta in italy, he said: *italschen*) &

the trigonometric point, the tall
wooden cross behind the house where
over the years the stones from
out of the fields had gathered. only there

would the travelling singer all nerves appear;
he would hoist his own scythe up &
then the fest began

culmitzsch

in the evening the sheep go rusty
over the wasted land, birds
as if snowed therein & darkened . . .

only under the rubble
the farmyards still are warm. the spoons
there by the spoons, the polish
by the boots & that little door
to the boot-room which moves you
to tears. *mother of spoons*

if i came back home all would be said.
your hamlet-bound walk, the
scabies, livestock, that knitting
against the tide & a smell
of resurrection in the air;

saltpetre thoughts, saltpetre discussions.
the pillow's moistness
beneath heads if they're still dreaming
    mushrooms of breath; the loam
    that ripples cool
    into my lungs when deep asleep . . .
good luck, good night
good mother of spoons, little princess of aprons; you

were never & from nothing illuminated, you
were radiant all on your own *good luck*
good night you drunken mothers. going home
    is a breath's contemplation
    a dusty turning back & softly

as if from afar the loam
falls back, slowly
from out of time into the straw & around
the invisible joints clings
a beam that erects itself
    alone, o

farm-ways into night's half-timbered frame.
dog deemed difficult, the home brew
    weighs heavy
birds' shadows
roll within the rubble;
this is the stone age of the villages

old garage question

did you go against the grating winter
(shovel on skull
moistness in bread
echo buried about the temples) did you

go against the grating winter
(a bird's turning-to-wood perched on
the laundry poles & hung
on the clothesline

the entire time) did you
go against the grating
winter (debt
stuck deep into
the old material & the anorak's
heavy hood hanging down, the growth
just like the raw ego) did you

go against the grating winter
& did you hold your little package all the way here
notch sharpened / script-hound harassed
straight through the rustling & sharp
as a knife that cuts waves
into little quotable pieces
    still who

will oil the bowden cable now? who
clean the carburettor needles
if they are not dead?

aranka, the name alone

fragile, a crackling
in wood, at her feet
the landscape's mechanics stood
out, a sound

of green spaces, well-worn paths, like
a barren bush rushing home
    on its branches that's
how she was beyond us, aranka

slippered, big calved, aranka, who
sang from out of the hollows of her knees, fists
on the wheelbarrow between the buckets, aranka

the name alone smells of bread
& leftovers—like
        worn-out angels' bodies
        on the run that's how she pulled

her wheelbarrow through
the wet grass beneath the laundry-poles, 'yeah,
    schälerelli, she's . . .
already eaten shit
for two marks'—i ask,

aranka, to where your weight has spread
which rustling or when

the emptiness in our voices began, the
pattering, stuttering & around

that stuttering
when it was the blocs & shadows grew
        like curses, where
as children we were put to sleep
        with an aluminium spoon in our mouths
        with a rubber hammer in our fists; only

from you, aranka,
not a single word. only
            the glistening fats, the juices
            of decay, alone
            in the dark your stinking wheelbarrow, its
grating whistling, that's how you set out. the wheel
was driven by a stick
& circled the house
of our sad origins' rest;

aranka, nights her glance would meet us
beneath the blanket, her toothless *o*
but do it sung from out of

the hollows of her knees, a hundred times over
the very same song: *aranka*

the name alone—
heat lightening from tristan sparrows

picked up & starved to death
in the electrical cabinet . . . aranka, once more:

forgive us!

the old company

had to come over the fields; we
(as far as we could) had armed ourselves &
been camped out for days in a hut
　　beneath the thorn-apple tree. in principle

we were well taken care of: sawyer, that
was me when finn didn't speak & finn
who immediately took over when
sawyer & i were silent. beyond that

there was the huge (as
we all imagined) deaf-mute black man who
came all the way from the branched & far-away
shafts below ronneburg

suddenly auntie lanny

suddenly auntie lanny comes to mind, she
who'd talk to us over
the fence, who'd talk

as if within a dream when we
ducked into the nettles.
almost accidental the way

one touches earth, a piece of wood, the
word follows the materials
like the old jewellery auntie lanny

threw out of her
bedroom window one morning for us
to play with—for ever

undecided, the
treasure of that time

hand-wonder & diary

my face wears its writing, my cheeks
are now clean. the man: long ago death
expressed himself with his bones. he
was the hand-miracle, the sorcerer
of all of culmitzsch & teichwolframsdorf.
slowly, like one comprehends a stone
we now sing his absence aloud.

whoever speaks, expires who
wanted to explain that: under chips, like
forgotten logs, frozen, nights
in the dark of the lamp . . . i'd take

those angst-steps into the courtyard where
      days his laughter
would hammer into the wood, his beckoning stutter, my
homeless heart; the man

was thin, bakelite, the man
was sugar-dusted, stiff-
necked, still
he cut every animal

into pieces & the head was nothing
without the limbs & the limbs
looked up at me curiously
from the table: in each & every animal

an old exhaustion was buried, hence
the auxiliary motor, the long shavings
        on the skin, back
& forth the time-shelves ('that's how
my first schnapps was & that's how
i took one through the arm . . .'); the man

with his little incurable foot
that had walked this land—'that
was good.' good like pebbles, good like weekdays in the debris;
        insertions, objections, overcooked daily . . . mornings

the man would wave his hand
over the STRADIVARI radio
in the kitchen behind my stool & everything
would stand at zero. the bright fresh

morning voices, gottschalk & the saint's days, the
        entire west, everything
as if waved back by his hand, the one that slowly
traversed the ether; i understood

only a clicking, a crackling, his otherworldly
laughter hammer into my
homeless heart: 'it's

        only my hand.' what a contrast
        the unique, tender transmission
        of his fingers' sound that in the end

would touch my head; i understood:
nothing, only a softly rustling hand; the man

an isotope, a crab
in a pot's shadow ('get
yourself some more butter, boy') & evenings
he would prick the white-
heads' grit from out of my face *i am*

the chopper illegal slaughterer meat inspector
with the finest of needles that
    returns to you now
right here above this table . . . elbows
resting, glasses uninhabited ('real still,
boy, please, still' or 'blood
plays no violin'—i
    thought about
abandoned figures, goofy, buratino,
pinocchio too with his head
in an inkwell) that's how he would prick

me in my face. the man—
i listened in on the rustling, the soft
current, the gas from the stove & a blue
crown that shivered in their yellow tips—'that
was a mistake.' mistake like *impure*, mistake
like *you*; i smelt
the dark amulet of animals
    from the pot, the soup

slowly stewing along
towards supper. first

i held out the left, then
the right, but the man
   extinguished me. he pricked
me in the face. every evening
a few small stones, lime
with fat & all the bad things

hissed fine when he carefully
directed the needle's point
into the candle; like
one who writes at night. mute at night
at the kitchen table. quietly in one's diary. someone
who's always known the text by heart & nevertheless
pauses, ever again, only *so*
     as not to spoil anything

into the mark

into the mark

i saw what the pines wrote
with their heavy snow hung
    bones; every sentence
was spun into sleep, the late
soundtrack for transport a fine
rustling of needles to the north. i

read cold freight documents. dreams
about wolves & desire, dreams
of dodona or swedenborg
where i've never been.

how do you call into the woods?
backwards over the eyes the echo *you*
    are all just steps, *chronically*
    in the atmosphere, *coronas of trees* that's how
    it comes back out.

exit saarmund—who thought *into the core*?
you loved the noise in the truck when
petrol streamed into the tank; i followed
the acrid smell of kennels in the air

why, antaeus, this place

shepherds' songs or army talk? mornings
in the moraines' evaporation voices walked
about the firs, idiot types, high insteps, playing

football with their dogs' bitten-through rubber
balls. i thought *piss brother babble* but
continued to listen & through my rigid
shadow grew a branch

& my hand, before this
wind from the moraines aslant,
wanted to wave, forever wave

the stay

one evening they came
the dead of my house
back from the train-station. one

after the other, with
balled fists, reminiscent
of tulips in their

night-reserve, reminiscent,
in the long being-dead, of all
the wasted time. from way back now

all's been theirs: every word, just
out of the lips, every good
sentence, as always

the home-made liverwurst, the
plum preserves, in addition
all the cigarettes & whatever

alcohol in reach. ceaselessly
they watched tv, ate chocolate (in huge
amounts) & whispered

verses to themselves. one evening
they came the dead of my house
back from the train-station. it was december &

their next train did not leave till march

october evening at the inflamed

maple tree on the street where
once again the *one who moved away*
is talking to the post-woman; with

them the wind & both
are holding their hands into the air—above
them a pair of branches

heaves a pine into the dream & a low
sun stands
on one of the truck's headlights

for Charlotta

do you see the redbrick moon

do you see the redbrick moon
above the eiffel towers? below that
the quacking, magnetic garbling & time
within the frogs' legs humming?

this is the old high-voltage lane. it
holds the moistness to the poles, holds
the fog & supports it. soft
blue shadows envelop all, a spider

hands away its threads & floats
as if electrified. dreams unearthed. endless
        intake when
the singing rises up the copper cables: o

people's song without a people & o
what thoughtepiphanies
evenings in the high-voltage lane

chaussee

the bast fibre's gone.
summit hard from long contact, written
empty. the

conical vase has tipped over, a farewell
text bespattered with filth in
a see-through jacket, freshly
fogged, indiscernible:

nope, no man, no boat from around here
not from this neck of the woods

the trains

i saw folded arms &
the conductor's glance
pale as old longing
drift out to us
from the side window. every friday at
five o'clock: the time when
the mechanics with
their machines rolled
slowly home; one
after the other, on every line
throughout the town so
long you had to wait at the
crossing there so long
that little by little your heart-
beat adapted itself
to the knocking, hammering, stamping, to
the whole almost desperate
rumbling & we all knew
to the gram
how much the dream weighed
pushed piece by piece
back into the track-bed

the glow of home

clear evenings walking.
the steps in the gravel
at one's feet once
again meet the stones'
mechanics.

the pond's called iris lake.
the street: at the train.
the moon-gazing algae's asleep
& lanterns
are dug into the ivy.

you still don't know
that you exist, & yet
what happens
is understood, in the brittle dark
the house it empties itself

autumn

is silence & custom. autumn
    is rake, wood, is a mild
    chill upon the eyes &

unexpected gooseflesh. is also
the good old ready-to-fight feeling, soft, secret, skull-still
designs maturing. the leaves all burnt, sand

still warm beneath the ashes, you
feel it now upon your hand: something
wants to flee & something never leave. so

one goes all the way
out back, behind the house. one falls
onto the grass & looks around:

globe-illumination, earth-rotation
across the neighbours' balconies. one
time home & return

it glistens from the dog-chains. 'my god
how the pine-tree tips are
suddenly red up top!' & under the earth

lie the dead
& hold the ends of the roots in their mouths

in the pipes

when water rushes in the pipes
        the house stands
still from listening. the
breath still comes, moves out &
        bit by bit
fatigue drags you back
by your feet; you

must underpin the weight
        of every word, all
that's underneath, an ear-guest
at your table. then you
feel the warm, flakey, carefully stored while
        up from out of the floor
a dead-mouse-smell, hipbones
like butterflies. now

the bell will be unclosed
an image round
by death composed

along i went, i froze

in field latin

in the nerve bundle of three birches:
existence silhouettes & old conventions
from the boughs like
    bogey man & soundless
    kilowatt consumer. all

the false partings, cleanly
traced within the archive
of slippery tradition. of course,

you say, it's the cold that
holds things hard in the eye, when
great stretches polish sleep
like angle grinders within
    the branches. one

also says: it's a tree
& wherever a tree stands so free
it has to speak

beware

as kids we always wanted
to march into other
countries, but
at the wood's edge were old
& had to turn back.

an eyeball the mother, an
eyeball the father;
& evenings when we had to go
    back home we
knew they both would roll

public news service

something down here sounds like dry
moss spanning the floor & your
footsteps announce your arrival. something

in the trees of cloud-german heroes laying
their shoulders against one another up there
in the sound. & something

stretches from the swing's push-
off point into the wish-frame
behind the doors, behind the light. everything
    is just as it seems

or smaller underway; which means:
'but he's from switzerland!'
'no, he's dead.'

sixth january

'but once, just after christmas, in the
        middle of the dream when
from out of the wardrobe my
polish alarm clock's sprained bell
suddenly began to sound,

three men carried the tree out of
the house. they scattered the gifts
across the snow &
next to them set up the tree. my bell

kept the beat of their sand-chamber hearts, the
branches supported their breath &
their mouths the hallelujah. that's how

they bowed, that's how they pardoned
the coming year, fleeting, staggering
under the shots

into their legs, arms, shoulders
while waving & disappearing
across the inner border'

along i went, i froze

along i went (in the woods), i felt
skin upon my head & a fine
abrasion of tide about my ears *were*

i another man . . . how quickly
all just thought again
forgot within the underbrush *once i was*

another: in hydesville, missouri
born. my daughter dolores
liked to clap her hands, she clapped & clapped &

one day something clapped back:
his name was splitfoot. dead
five years before—'another man'

so ran the theme of this going—hard
in the ether, soft in the ear, good material
for those at home at their poems, but also

for all those who alone
(so damn alone)
are outside there & listening

what we see

the question sounds; fingers
distress the snow a little along
an icy thought—what

we see, the question sounds
high up in the trees. it's even
what they talk about. the now & again

rolls up over the eyes with an
endearingly flexible suspension, utterly
intimate & unfathomable

wasn't that the way? indeed

that's where you wanted to live, there
where one after the other they
disappeared without a word, nothing left

but the air-dried & later cold-
filled mirror traces, there
where step by step things are completed & blessed

one after the other, something
always pulled you to that promise, there
another wind blew, a still storm you
constantly drove past & yet

still felt in your face for real, a
second life, a piece of earth, it was ready
for you & for the off chance
you might ever stop: with brown herbs

a silence would grow into your mouth &
upon those thistles'
tips good words, sweet & savoury, a
tonality up on capillaries

from out of the depths & on the off chance
you might stop: you would take these boards, these ditches

& step by step touch
this or that piece

of this perfectly abandoned place

early animal

it's the comforting face of moss
now upside down the earth-
lined rooting

of the eyes the
good brown net of nerve endings
grasps into the air as if

not having understood & on
the capillary remains of
a suddenly scattered thought

sits the bird
alone with his worm

what i possessed

within the fields' rippling script the glimmer
of a few glass bricks, some tufts of grass & the small
    rests of bones: how

it all lies together in the end.
arise, ascent & so there was
a lot of signalling, radioing, failure
about my feet, step after step. hood

down tight across my ears, my
arms ringing, the fine
scraping work of my coat, over
back, back & over—my

very own quarter in which to creep.
the going slow was softer &
standing still just once
i almost died

as far as africa

bodmers vale

in the beginning when
    from behind the wind
blasts into the skins & opens
the tiny bodies. when

the mask snaps & stitch by
stitch the seams burst
in the middle of your face—not

a good sight. when
the years, wood
& bone-growth branch
    off, stones
roll into the sinews & stars

give way to draft—
'not a good scene!' &
in zurich hard to believe

the photographer & his motifs

is it to the rod-ends' wavering
light the souls
spring up from out of the water while
the fishermen sleep? no. once

upon a time: a simple house & a
simple house peered from out of my
eyes. journey

underway within me, the street
like going through rooms
    at evening already, traces
read hard into the carpet. but

now the fairytale's gone. every shot
dives back into his eye &
has truly earned it & together
they're tired & sleeping

fall prey
to every fisherman's net

darss poem

the woods whisper into the sea ahead.
a few of my giants are bent
    into two & splinter
still there grinding. their leaves

harden slow & hang
tight upon the branches, they hang
turn to metal & hang. that's

how the never-said's
    entwined
behind the back in hands; i think

i'd only need the old quiet
    beneath my hood, only
my hands, a bit of wind
at my back to drive my feet, to drive
the man on his way down the beach
through history, indeed:

i've already slept through the
spinney, the water-level, the harbour, now
let us be on our way

the river elbe near wilsnack

we waded a few steps out into the
water. about our feet
eddies & streets, on
the pavement algae like slender
swerving temples, free from having to think.

that was good. around our ankles
the water eased & spoke
in ancient tongues:
'you really can't have it all'
'you really can only do one thing'
'what has three legs can stand.'

that was enough. in the river's middle
the word *swallow-bottle* flowed:
fist-sized hollows
of loam on the lock
where they live like animals. then

space lost me. i saw
the fine excavation of dust
cover the voice, the fine
    lint, the soft
needles' sloughing between
skin and skin *play*

that old vinyl again the
record with the childlike
cries up from below, the courtyard, that meeting
right before leaving
for a much better place. meanwhile

upstairs the old guy's chewing his cantos & the dust
between your fingers
it still feels like remembering

paternity

he embodied something
for me & i
embodied him in himself. i sat

instead of him at the wheel on
the backseat my children
embodied me & i

in their place in
his back
thought of

sticky leather telegraphing sleeping
the drifting sky
in the back of wonder white

    zhiguli

anecdote from the last war

barracks 6 has taken up post:
'the man in the last row, bottom right
has laughed too much.'

& now, soldier, let us consider
the blackness of this about-face, the
many poorly made stops & starts
we can read here as if printed
by boots, polish, leather: let us read
& consider the false
steps of an entire class, impressed
there on the linoleum. the traces of whistle-blown
dreams, battle alarms' shorthand, readings
all the way to the arms depot. & now
spell out the corridor, soldier, all
the way to your room: sharp
legs, almost cyrillic. in contrast
to the blunt ends &
niebelungen-deep *as far as it seems*
executed by bent bones, only
an orthopaedic hieroglyph. from what's been translated
we understand:

when this is the text, you are the man
with pail, water, blade, shaving kit in hand

to the sky

with the first flakes
the marvellous falls back
into open mouths. the
ungraspable: it tastes

like nothing, but something
sounds in the chest & passes
to the tongue *the soft
hiss of the snow*. & so

every un-beheaded dream
awakes & my tilted skull
pulls me pure white
flaked darkness & on

the roof of my mouth's a
melted mass of sweet lust
i soar up into this realm

mylius street

at night the house stretched itself
slowly out through the
curtains. in the corners of its eyes

lanterns too & shadows
as if carved into plaster: a general assembly
of wasted hours. from door to door
the little fluffed-up ivy beds, the
drains in the grass glittered like
       gravestones, so fresh
you almost didn't want to breathe
when walking past . . . but surely

that's only mylius street. the
wolkenstein society, weigand—internal medicine.
hely real estate, hartmann/partner, the burda-center &

the clara schumann house number 32. i
only saw the venetian blinds, the lock
       in the back, how
iron slowly ages in the latch. at

eye-level an insect, pressing
its stomach to the warm window—i
quietly asked through the glass: whither the way?
the slow space-flight of his steps passed away

exit sangerhausen—as if

you were at home here too. & over
    there outside as well where
the light pierces through & straight
down's made up of layers of cloud: accounts

of major laundry, bath day, *wolleyball*
on the drying area. 'during advent alone
student s. collected eighty-two bottles
for africa.' the one-armed shop teacher: making
a floral lamp, for weeks at a time, he showed us, using

the vice as a hand. exit
sangerhausen; if only
you ever stopped: each blade of grass would bow & offer
up its pallid story. a pair of unforgotten leaves would waft
down the street & wind

their clocks on concrete. & above you
there'd be birds, long untouched by anything
at all & higher still, a crooked
bit of grace, in the rain, its feet

turned inwards to africa

for Einar Schleef

footonauts

'They were fine, my companions, they never complained
about the work or the thirst or the frost,
they had the bearing of trees and waves
that accept the wind and the rain
accept the night and the sun
without changing in the midst of change.'

George Seferis, 'The Argonauts'

the footonauts

dedicated to my soccer friends

sometimes they too sang. those were
the tiergarten years when
we played in front of the reichstag. later, exiled already
we took to playing in wedding, barfuß street, schiller park. almost
a barren field, totally turkish, the drone
in our heads, the boeings that sank toward tegel. so

we retreated. all the way to potsdam, there
everything was nice: a turf, shade, post-
game swims in the holy lake. we left a lot of
capes behind us. we
          would swim past both
of gunter jauchs' villas. sit
out on the shore, a table & the terraces
in front of villa kellermann. the sun
would go down. the smell of evening come, hair slowly
drying on our necks. surrounded by castles
          & gardens. not to mention the wheat beer,
asparagus, post-game analyses—all in all: the lush

          life. until
something came from out of the bushes' shadows: something
from out of the strange & lowest city departments. what
drove us away from this last
magical meadow, wieland street, once hitler-ring. still

we bravely held on
in potsdam, from paradise far. a hard public
    field, a dreary
island, dreary beach, where fine festering sand endlessly laid
into
    fresh wounds. that's how
legs age, arms age, thursday
after thursday. we saw
good men sink at the knees. then
escape: the noble clearing, a forested pitch toward michendorf. we
set forth—still we found no people, there

we lacked adversaries. companions, eyes
    sunken, tired from all the searching
attendant to failing, moved back to berlin. a
street by the name of forckenbeck:
the name was that of a prussian manor house, but the field
            was english, like
one last passion so full & thick & short, beautiful & almost
unreal. the groundskeeper, prussian again, spoke:
'nothing with cleats, boy, take your shoes off!' i never
saw the man again. we often asked, we still don't know—
is the groundskeeper dead already or was his position
simply eliminated? space gone to seed, the fleece
dulled—these voyages, must they be endless?

still, i quietly ask myself, weren't
my companions' souls, haven't our bodies
already long been one with this place's

sober face? worn down by scars, furrows,
the dark? the season was great, the games
          good, whither
now the way—dear friends
how long must we still flee? dear winfried, hendrik, peter, carsten,
dear michael, tobias, jan—
this time, please, let us stay: bellow, trot, scream at goals
& launch passes, let us
      carry one or two more good balls over this
            our very last field

(1990–2005)

inventory

inventory

you've investigated time
in the lamphead: branches, two building-
rows, already dusted off word for word.
all is open up to the eyes—who

said that? i sit here now as if
written myself, pencil on
paper. the gas meter ticks, one
drinks oneself tight for this text & has

the wrong punctuation in the blood. over there
the bottles on the oven, here
the wood chips, half chewed to bits, the smell
of the freshly sawn—every

character scrapes the things
back into your bones through graphite, only
you never get any closer to crying

the very first affection

the shadows, aged early, but we
remember: homeward, lonely
simply walking
step by step recording
the silent outline. for

the shadows, at the beginning,
were the small, black units of pay
a currency for which
the creator interrupted his
    work. one

after the other he carefully stretched
down & lined
along the scaly empty row. only HE
    would so tenderly
place it on the crowns of our heads: salvation

& its long conception starts
at the hairline, what's called
the world's very first affection. there
where that dark corner, that lint-
like overflow
sprang from the skull *like being reborn*

the creator thought
  & pulled it out
    & set it straight
     & easily laid it down
over the back again, way back
into the destiny of the lantern-ways. earlier

we ran into our shadows'
neck & he toppled
helplessly over the points of our woollen caps
into the abyss. but today

we remember:
simply walking, electric light
   & something at the crown of the head
when we stand
beneath a lantern

may the south save us

when walking he constantly held his hands
folded to the inside so
as to keep his jacket's ever-
cascading arms from
falling off his shoulders; nothing

is more ridiculous than a man
walking without any hands, nothing worse
than love's evaporation
into sudden laughter—

may the south save us, thought the man
& once again folded his hands

end

could be that was not our end, only
the pause, just like a silence
can slip suddenly into talk. we

were waiting for wind & chill, but
wind & chill did not arrive. could be
i stayed silent too loud, i breathed

into the candlelight & a sleeping insect
burnt, everything, its wings, feeler
legs, everything bristled once again,

came into order, glistened, &
in the flame, fine, a face
swollen up with eyes

whoever walks behind

whoever walks behind
has their own world. softly
everything falls from the
sound of their steps
up into the leaves. you hear

the dragging, scraping, shuffling
of their legs into
the unwritten centre
with steps that merely stumble on
when they close

their eyes in the back
the mountains set off with them
from their existence
full of caverns, rivers, peaks at
their feet, who-

ever walks behind strides across the day
that you've forgotten
their own day, their own world
which they cover with steps all the
way through the scenes of your struggles, who-

ever walks behind has misplaced themselves, ear
in the seam, a gentle echo on the soles, they
are the trace-sleepers upon the way

that stretches them inside, long
overfilled with things that

didn't know how to go on—who-
ever walks behind teeters & sings
& even calls the dog
you're whistling off
into their soft, substantial silhouette

whereas your own way it suffers
fixed-costs & twilight

come on mum make

come on mum make
me the bone ladder look
i've got a lovely bunch of
school-teeth now all of them i

already have some tear-
liquids too like ground
jewels in the face i am

so all alone here by me, no, i mean
by myself i know *and you* stood
on the ground without a light &
cut out from thoughts from thinking o

wonder what
helped us up from out of need but
not up from out of this mud

night drive

just between us, which meant quietly
as far as the windshield
on this the way from i to you
    dejected, dreaming
over streets, routes, long projected
travel plans—

'do you hear the knuckle-
bones of my dead knocking
there in the dark?'
'do you hear the rats & their
quick light strides
circle the earth's core in the night?'

quietly as far as the windshield—
on this way everything falls
back into its weight & the freshly
whitewashed country road
lies under banks of fog; alone

the child who always sits in back
the child in the rearview mirror is
the last one still to count
& silently speak to himself—head

pressed down to arm
he keeps his eyes shut tight
till everything takes flight

hypnotized modern

'the hoof went high, the heat-carnation
had already climbed out
of the mouth, ashen . . .' shut it, writer. with
intonation trees once more are trees, mills
screwed up with stones, birds
tilt far away in the air
with markings on
            their legs: move it

writer. open the window.
eyes straight ahead what
do you see? you see seriously
disappointed hot-air balloons above alaska, no
one able to land, propeller-
planes, endless flight . . . *writer*

what i thought, hidden in
leather-rust i spoke
into the field-grey of my blanket: are you holding
your ears still in the light? are you following
in your lamp's thread while
button for button the brown earth

falls from your bones? for fleeing hares
            aphorisms are enough. still

whoever marches from the heart or hard liver

his foxtrot through to the hips, all the way

to vorkuta, touches

the earth's axis with hidden strides

swings a root with

his feet, a burnt

smell in the leaves: *dictations*

       writer. *show* what

among them stands below

his burnt-off writing hand:

       a dried-out drag mark? a laughable

       copy of the odyssey? nothing but this

       thin, field-service-mail-

like writing scratched into paper? is that

verse? a calligraphy

       for the poor? that

from the tip of the expired fuse nothing

but coals falls out? *shut it, writer*. first

the cut. the blood

     comes later, feel how

snow holds silence & pulls the strings

in the storm; writer: take over

as if

sinking in, a whispering to:
from out of the old wiring you still spark
between the stations.
you shuffle through conversations

in the leaves, through the voices
in the rustling, heard
from outside, passing by: that's how
you remain standing. night

starts at the house, tongue
in the seam, the unsaid
in eyes. as if

you had written
everything properly. as if
you had already died

the scent of poems

'concentrate, pretty please!' that
was the sound of our long
⠀⠀⠀sunday mornings &
her liturgy: glove, the cranes
of ibykus, john maynard
was our helmsman, all the same

my mother set the course:
line for line, the author's
name, title, a small
pause & then the poem:
enjambment, a term that
no one knew, only the ladle

to direct me, the teeter & nod
over the pots with dumplings
& thuringian sauce, first
the words, then the points ('the
commas too are not for nothing') & then
my mother's most inner emotions which
came to me—i

stood in the kitchen doorway, i learnt it
all from her: first without the stress
then with

the end will come in the stairwell

the end will come: it wasn't you.
that was not you
discovered

faint, the accidental
victim of a timer-circuit *relay*
like something suddenly on

& suddenly off again, so that
endlessly tired stumbling (flickering) you
climbed up & down in front of the doors,

names, bell-scrawl in the nothingness
'i' & 'he' & 'we' inhabit. with-
out any purpose, without resembling

any real people at all

Notes

the new empire
The title of this poem echoes the title of Stefan George's final collection of poetry *Das neue Reich* (Berlin: Georg Bondi, 1928).

'chandos hysteria' is a reference to Hugo von Hofmannstahl's fictional letter entitled 'Letter to Lord Chandos' first published in 1902 in Berlin's newspaper *Der Tag* (The Day). Many critics considered it one of the first primary texts of the new century. The Modernism Lab at Yale writes:

In the letter, Lord Chandos claims that he is experiencing a crisis of language that has rendered him unable to write as he has written in the past. A great deal of the analysis of the work has focused on the apparent paradox that, despite claiming to be unable to write, the author composes a letter of considerable length and never fully explains the source of the crisis of language.

'come in / to the research park / they say is dead' is a reference to Stefan George's famous poem of 1895, 'komm in den totgesagten park und schau' (come into the park they say is dead and see). [Trans.]

harvest fest
Luftwaffe or German air-force. Italschen is Saxon/Thuringian dialect for 'Italy'. [Trans.]

culmitzsch
Culmitzsch was a village in the Bundesland (federal state) of Thuringia, one of the five states that once comprised the communist German Democratic Republic or East Germany (1949–90). Culmitzsch's inhabitants were forcibly removed and relocated to make room for one of the largest uranium mines in the former

GDR. Environmental degradation complete, the village was definitively razed in 1970. [Trans.]

old garage question

The final line of the poem, 'and if they are not dead' echoes the traditional ending of German fairytales: 'und wenn sie nicht gestorben sind / dann leben sie noch heute' (and if they are not dead / they live there still). [Trans.]

the old company

Ronneburg is a small town in Thuringia. During the time of the GDR, according to some estimates, as much as 11 per cent of the world's uranium was mined there. [Trans.]

hand-wonder & diary

Teichwolframsdorf is part of a rural Thuringian municipality. Stradivari was a type of radio. Gottschalk refers to radio and television personality Thomas Gottschalk. [Trans.]

into the mark

In Dodona, the oldest oracle of the Greek world, prophecies were foretold by listening to the rustling of trees. Homer called the male priests Selloi. However, the criteria they used were unclear even to contemporaries. [LS]

The Mark Brandenburg is an informal way of referring to the federal state of Brandenburg. Though Brandenburg surrounds the city of Berlin, it is a separate state. Brandenburg's capital, Potsdam, is about 15 miles southwest of Berlin and was once the residence of Prussian royalty and later the site of the Potsdam Conference, which decided the shape of post–Second World War Europe. Saarmund is a borough in the county Potsdam-Mittelmark of Brandenburg. [Trans.]

in field latin

Though none of these poems are explicitly referred to, perhaps it is interesting, as Walter Fabian Schmid has written, to consider the poem within the following continuum. In 1939, Bertolt Brecht wrote: 'Ah, what an age it is / When to speak of trees is almost a crime / For it is a kind of silence about injustice!' (Bertolt Brecht, *Selected Poems* [H. R. Hays trans.] [New York: Reynal &Hitchcock, 1947], p. 173). Later, Gunter Eich was to write: 'The chestnuts bloom. / I take it in, / but feel no need to comment' (Gunter Eich, *Gesammelte Werke, Bd. I* [Frankfurt am Main: Suhrkamp, 1973], p. 166 [this translation by Alexander Booth]). Walter Helmut Fritz, in his 1976 poem 'Trees', had this to say: 'In the meantime it has / almost become a crime / not to speak about trees' (Alexander Booth trans.). In 'A Leaf, Treeless' Paul Celan wrote: 'What times are these / when a conversation / is almost a crime / because it includes / so much made explicit?' (Paul Celan, 'A Leaf, Treeless', in *Poems of Paul Celan* [Michael Hamburger trans.] [London: Anvil, 1988], pp. 330–1). [Trans.]

along i went, i froze

On 11 April 1848, Margaret Fox swore that the sounds of knocks were to be heard in her house in Hydesville, New York. Something was responding to the clapping of her youngest daughter's hands. The family believed they were in contact with a certain Mr Splitfoot, a former inhabitant who had died five years before: 'Mr Splitfoot does as I do, clapping his hands.' In the years following the implementation of Samuel B. Morse's telegraph (between Washington and Baltimore), the knocking in the Fox household became a point of departure for a great number of reports of 'spiritual telegraphing'. [LS]

bodmers vale
Karl Bodmer (1809–93) was a Swiss painter. He accompanied
Maximilian Prinz zu Wied on an expedition into the interior of
North America in 1832 and documented the journey with his
drawings. Watercolours of Indian dances emerged as well as por-
traits of chiefs and warriors. [LS]

the photographer & his motif
The poem was inspired by the photograph 'Strassenfotograf' by
Robert Häusser. [LS]

darss poem
Darss is a small half-island located in the Mecklenburg-Western
Pomerania region of the Baltic Sea. Its name is said to derive from
old Slavic and means 'place of thorns'. [Trans.]

the river elbe near wilsnack
When years ago I first heard the recordings of Ezra Pound reading
his Canto 106, I thought that the bright, happy voices in the
background were those of playing children. In my mind's eye I
saw a courtyard from which the voices rose to the room of he who
was reading. Only later did I learn that the recording had been
done in the psychiatric clinic of St Elizabeth's Federal Hospital in
Washington DC, where Pound had been sent after the war. In fact,
they are the cries of patients ever-resounding through the corridors
while 'the old guy chews his cantos'. [LS]

paternity
Zhiguli was the name given to the Lada VAZ 2101 automobile
designed primarily for countries of the Eastern bloc by FIAT and
produced in Russia between 1970 and 1988. It is not to be confused
with the East German–produced Trabant. [Trans.]

mylius street
Mylius Street is located in the Hessian city of Frankfurt. [Trans.]

exit sangerhausen—as if
Sangerhausen is a town in the German state of Saxony-Anhalt whose capital is Magdeburg. Einaar Schleef (1944–2001) was, among other things, a German writer, photographer and theatre director from Sangerhausen. About him the Nobel Prize–winning Austrian writer Elfriede Jelinek has said: 'In Germany after the War there have only been two geniuses: [Rainer Werner] Fassbinder in the West, and Schleef in the East.' [Trans.]

the footonauts
The English translation of 'Argonauts' by George Seferis appears in *George Seferis: Collected Poems 1924–1955* (Princeton, NJ: Princeton University Press, 1982) (pp.). [Trans.]

In 2003, the Footonauts' hopes to return to the grass before the Reichstag building, the starting point of their 15-year odyssey, were definitively dashed. After the complaints of parliamentarians, a ban on ball playing was issued. [LS]

'until something came from out of the bushes' shadow': representatives of the Lower Parks & Green Spaces Commission. [LS]

The Reichstag is the seat of the German Parliament in Berlin. Wedding is an area of Berlin, after the Second World War located within the French sector. Tegel is Berlin's largest airport. Gunther Jauch is a famous showman, journalist and producer. Michendorf is a small area about nine kilometres south of Potsdam. [Trans.]

come on mum make
In the German version, a couple of phrases are borrowed from a children's poem by August Heinrich Hoffmann von Fallersleben,

interestingly enough, the man who also composed the German national anthem (though this fact has nothing to do with the poem). There is, however, no similar echo to be had in English. [Trans.]

hypnotized modern

Vorkuta is a Russian town located north of the Arctic Circle and was the site of one of the Gulag's largest forced labour camps. On account of charges of 'anti-Soviet agitation' and espionage, the German writer Horst Bienek (1930–90) was sent to Vorkuta; the German journalist Horst Schüler (1924) was also sent there after having been convicted in 1951 of similar charges. The last phrase in the German version of the poem, 'schreiber: übernehmen sie' echoes the German title ('Kobra, übernehmen Sie') of the US television series *Mission Impossible*. [Trans.]

the scent of poems

'The Cranes of Ibycus' is a poem by Friedrich Schiller (Tübingen: JG Cotta, 1798). 'John Maynard' is a poem by Theodor Fontane (Munich: Verlagsanstalt für Kunst und Wissenschaft, 1886). [Trans.]

Translator's Acknowledgements

Firstly, my warmest thanks to Seagull Books for their interest and trust.

Next, at Suhrkamp Verlag I would like to thank Petra Hardt, Doris Plöschberger, Thomas Sparr and, *vor allem*, Nora Mercurio for her tireless dedication, engagement and friendship. May the gods of poetry continue to bless them all.

I am extremely grateful to my mother Irmgard for her patience, not least with readings, and for helping to clarify a number of points on early drafts. My thanks to Petra Nass for her help and friendship, and to Katharina Erben for her indispensable care, comments and suggestions as well as, in a certain sense, having helped me to begin this project.

I would next like to thank Timothy Barnes, Brian Freeman, Peter Lerner, Craig Peritz, Nicholas Stanley-Price and Francesca Toticchi for their long friendship and support.

Grateful acknowledgement and thanks is due to the PEN American Center and its committee for supporting my project by selecting it for a 2012 Heim Translation Fund grant and for publishing one of those poems in their PEN Journal. I would also like to thank David and Helen Constantine at Modern Poetry in Translation, Aditi Machada at Asymptote, Jim Hicks at Massachusetts Review, Joshua Mensch at BODY and Nia Davies at Poems in Which and Poetry Wales for having selected a number of these poems to publish. A special note of thanks to Paola del Zoppo at Del Vecchio Editore for her kindness and friendship as well.

Finally, I would like to thank Lutz Seiler for his humility and kindness and for sharing his singular gift of sentiment, sight and song.